Pawtographs

The CRAZY KIDS GUIDE TO COOKING FOR YOUR PET

By CRAZY DOG

WHO ELSE COULD WRITE A PET COOKBOOK?

Featuring
The **Back Bones** of **Character**™

Characters Building Character™

Crazy Pet Press

Translated by
Barbara & Missy Denzer
Illustrated by
Manny Rodriguez

A Word from the Prez

The mission of the Crazy Pets is to present edutainment: humorous and fun learning activities for children (of all ages) that create ways for them to interact with their pets - or their imaginary pets - and to teach and reinfor "The Back Bones of Character" through the Crazy Pet cartoon characters. (Not bad for a bunch of cartoon pets, huh?)

BaBY DOG®   CRaZY DOG®   CRaZY Cat®   CRaZY
                                                         LittLe Kitty

The Rules:
All rights are reserved. No part of this book may be reproduced without written permission from the top dog, except for reviewers who may quote brief passages or reproduce illustrations in a review with appropriate credits (provided it's a positive review). Don't let us catch you reproducing part of this book, storing it in some kind of retrieval system or transmitting it in any form or by any means (electronic, mechanical, photocopying, recording or other) without written permission from Crazy Spike, chief of security, or he'll have to bite your leg off.

©2003 Crazy Pet Press. Crazy Dog® Baby Dog® Crazy Cat® Crazy Little Kitty®, Characters Building Character™ The Back Bones of Character™ and Play With Your Pets, Care For Your Pets™ are licensed trademarks of Crazy Pet LLC. Azusa, CA. Pet Botanics® and Ear Mite & Tick Control® are trademarks of Cardinal Laboratories Inc. Azusa, C. Used by permission.

Published in San Ramon, CA by The Crazy Pet Press. www.crazypetpress.com

First Edition. All Rights Reserved. Printed in Korea.

Denzer, Barbara Bedell & Missy Denzer, The Crazy Kids Guide to Cooking For Your Pet

Illustrated by Manny Rodriguez

With special thanks to Tony de Vos for his vision, support and encouragement.

Library of Congress Control Number: 200309 6396

ISBN Number: 0-9744749-0-8

Age levels: 6 and up.

The Crazy Kids Guide to Cooking For Your Pet
Featuring The Back Bones of Character
Recipes, Cartoons, Jokes, Pet Care Tips & Fun Things

Table of Contents

Building character is part of growing up - and taking care of your pet.

Crazy Dog's Back Bones of Character™

BE CARING
- Have Concern & Compassion
- Help Others, Take Care of Your Pets
- Be Good, Friendly, Generous
- Listen & Share Feelings

CONTRIBUTE
- Volunteer, Join Clubs
- Make Your World Better
- Care for the Environment
- Be An Example of Good Character

HAVE COURAGE
- Tell the Truth
- Be Loyal & Honest
- Stand Up for What's Right
- Make Good Choices

BE DEPENDABLE
- Keep Promises
- Be On Time
- Show Up When You Commit
- Do A Job Right

BE FAIR
- Follow the Rules
- Share
- Take Turns
- Treat Everyone the Same

HAVE RESPECT
- Talk, Think & Act Positive
- Be Considerate and Courteous
- Follow The Golden Rule
- Do Not Make Fun of Anyone

Characters Building Character ™

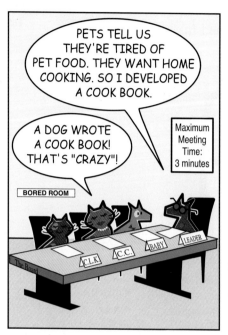

Dog Treat Recipes

A FUN THING YOU CAN DO WITH YOUR DOG:

Have a birthday party for your dog. Invite some neighborhood dogs. Let them play together. Plan some fetch games. Make party hats, place mats and place cards. Make a birthday cake. Go to www.crazydog.com to print out things you can use for your party. Make a cake from our simple Birthday Cake recipe found on page 19!

Cheezzy Dog Bones

Ingredients:

2 c.	All Purpose or Wheat Flour
1/2 t.	Minced Fresh Garlic or Garlic Powder
1 1/3 c.	Shredded Cheddar Cheese
1/2 c.	Canola Oil
4-5 T.	Water

Combine ingredients and mix well to form a stiff dough, kneading slightly. Flour surface and pat or roll into a thick square. Cut out with a bone shaped cookie cutter. Or use a paper bone shaped pattern to cut around. Bake in a pre-heated oven at 400 degrees for 15-18 minutes, until slightly brown on the bottom. Cool completely. Store in sealed sandwich bags.

Tested by Wheely Willy and his owner Deborah Turner co-author of How Willy Got His Wings. Visit www.wheelywilly.com to see his books and learn his story.

DOGS LOVE CHEESE

✓ PET CARE TIP
Make sure your pet always wears an I.D. Tag with his name and your name and phone number on it.

Frozen Pup-Cakes

Ingredients:

6   Cheese Slices – at room temperature

1   Large Can of Your Dog's Favorite Dog Food

6 t.   Peanut Butter

Take a cupcake pan and place a slice of cheese in each cup, pushing down to form the shape of the pan. Fill the cheese in the cup with about 1/2 c. of canned dog food. Fold any excess cheese over the top of the dog food. Garnish with one teaspoon of peanut butter on top. Put the cupcake pan in the freezer and wait 3-4 hours or overnight. Let your dog sample a non-frozen one while you clean up. Now, clean up after your dog!

"Groomer of the Century"
Dina Perry and her standard poodle Skeeter loved
this one!!! Together they run Wag'n Tails Pet Resort in Lansing, Michigan
and work as representatives for Wag'n Tails Mobile Conversions in Granger, Ind.

DOGS LOVE PEANUT BUTTER

CATS DON'T.

PEANUT BUTTER

✓ PUPPY CARE TIP
Puppies aren't coordinated enough to catch flying saucer toys. Wait until they're older so they don't get hurt while their bones and muscles are forming.

Hot Diggity Dogs

Ingredients:

1/2 c.	Flour
1 can	**Solid** Dog Food (no sauce*)
1 c.	Peanut Butter
1/2 c.	Sour Cream
1 T.	Chicken Bouillon for flavor
1 1/2 c.	Crumbled Dry Dog Food

Put the dry dog food in a sandwich bag and use an ice cream scoop or heavy spoon to crush into crumbs. Put crumbs in a small dish or saucer and put aside.

Put the first 5 ingredients in a large bowl and mix well. When everything is thoroughly mixed, take a handful of the mixture and form it into hot dog shapes. Roll the hot dogs in the crumbs and then place on a cookie sheet. Bake at 325 degrees for 15-20 minutes. Cool well before serving to your pet.

* If your brand of dog food does have sauce, you'll need to add 1/2 to 1 cup more flour.

This recipe was tested by Marea Tully,
Intl. Grooming Consultant for Andis Company,
with the help of her two granddaughters, Robyn and Maya,
Standard Poodle, Tivi and Miniature Schnauzer Ruthie wagged their
tails so hard and knocked over their bowls in delight over their new treat.

KID ALERT!
Do not feed Hot Diggity Dogs to your pet skunk - or he's sure to raise a stink!

☑ DOG CARE TIP
Dogs drink lots of water. Always have a big bowl of clean, fresh water where your dogs can help themselves. When you take them some place make sure you bring some water and a dish with you!

A FUN THING YOU CAN DO WITH YOUR DOG:
Teach your dog simple tricks. Visit www.crazydog.com to learn how to teach your dog to sit, rollover and fetch.

Hush Puppies
(Shareables)

(If your puppy's whining 'cause he's teething, this will hush him up.)

Ingredients:

2 c. Dry Oatmeal or Quick Oats
2 c. Creamy or Chunky Peanut Butter

Put the 2 cups of oatmeal in a mixing bowl. Add 2 cups of peanut butter and stir well with a spoon or wooden spoon until the oatmeal clumps into a big ball.

Scoop out a large spoonful of the mixture and roll into a small ball. Place the balls on a cookie sheet and freeze 3-4 hours or until hard. Remember, these are for your puppy, you have to ask him if he'll share with you!

Tested by Anna Moore, 8, and Camille Montenegro, 9, of Chino Hills California, for Anna's dog Toby.

I DON'T WANT TO SHARE MY HUSH PUPPIES!

SHARING IS PART OF BEING FAIR.

DOGS LOVE THEIR FAMILY

BE FAIR

✓ DOG CARE TIP

If you are attending training or agility classes with your pet – always have a play time after a training session to reward them for their hard work.

KID ALERT!

Let sleeping dogs lie. Dogs don't like to be disturbed when they're sleeping.

BABY DOG®

DOGS LOVE

THEIR OWN BED

HAVE RESPECT

Let Your Dog Sleep.

Lolli-Pups
(Cousins of Hush Puppies)

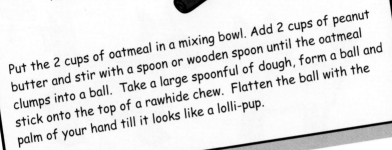

Ingredients:

2 c.	Dry Oatmeal or Quick Oats
2 c.	Creamy or Chunky Peanut Butter
	Rawhide Chews

Put the 2 cups of oatmeal in a mixing bowl. Add 2 cups of peanut butter and stir with a spoon or wooden spoon until the oatmeal clumps into a ball. Take a large spoonful of dough, form a ball and stick onto the top of a rawhide chew. Flatten the ball with the palm of your hand till it looks like a lolli-pup.

Tested by Professional Groomer,
educator and pet product manufacturer John Stazko,
Tori (5) and Brian (4). Their dog said Lolli-pups are "g-r-r-r-ate!"
Mom says let the kids roll Lolli-pups in a little bit of powdered sugar for their own treat.

PET CARE TIP

Playing games with your pet helps them develop their body movements and that makes them smarter and more coordinated!

Happy Birthdog Cake

Ingredients:

Cut one 3" slice of Pet Botanics® Lamb & Brown Rice Meat Roll to make the "cake". Place it on a fancy birthday paper plate. (Take a plain paper plate and decorate it with markers.)

3 TB peanut butter - spread on "cake" for frosting

Rawhide Sticks - use for candles. One stick for every year. Every year in our calendar is roughly the equivalent of 7 years for a dog. If your dog has one "candle" he's actually 7 dog years old!

Make your dog a birthday hat!

DOGS LOVE PARTIES!

✓ DOG CARE TIP

Many dogs are sent to the shelter because they aren't trained to be a good pet. Dogs and people are both happier if dogs are well trained. People have to be taught how to train their pets to make them good members of the family. If you have a dog, enroll in a dog training class and learn how to train your dog, or call a professional dog trainer.

✓ DOG CARE SAFETY TIP

Some pets love to travel with you but cars quickly turn into ovens in the summer and freezers in the winter. If you take your pet with you in your car, take your pet with you when you get out of the car (otherwise leave them at home).

Lazy Logs

For Lazy Kids Who Want Their Dogs to Think They Worked Soooo Hard to Make Them a Treat

Ingredients:

6   Rawhide Sticks

1   3.5 oz. Bag of Crazy Dog Train Me! treats

Some Peanut Butter

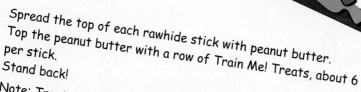

Spread the top of each rawhide stick with peanut butter. Top the peanut butter with a row of Train Me! Treats, about 6 per stick.

Stand back!

Note: Treat your dog to one stick, put the rest in the freezer for a day when you're feeling even lazier than today!

WE MIGHT BE CRAZY...

BUT WE'RE NOT LAZY!

✓ **PUPPY CARE TIP**
Puppies lose their puppy teeth
and cut new teeth just like you do.
That's why they're always chewing on things.
Make sure your puppy has rawhide bones,
chews, hard biscuits or sturdy rubber toys
to chew on during teething – or make them some
of your frozen treats!

Meat-O Eat-Os

(Basic Meatball recipe)

Ingredients:

1#	Hamburger meat
1 c.	Dry Dog Food
1 c.	Wheat Germ
1/4 c.	Canola Oil
1/4 c.	Creamy Peanut Butter
1 c.	Beef Broth or Water
1/4 c.	Pet Botanics® Skin & Coat Supplement - or flour

Put the cup of dry dog food in a large storage bag and seal it. Smash the dry food into crumbs by hitting the bag with the back of a big spoon or putting it on the floor (on a newspaper) and stepping on it. When you have crumbs, take out about a Tablespoon of the dry mix and put on a saucer.

Now put the dry mix and all the other ingredients in a bowl and mix together well. Take spoonfuls of meat and form into meatballs with your hands. Roll them in the dry mix - so they won't stick to a pan or cookie sheet. Put the meat balls into a pan in the freezer for at least 4 hours before serving. Keep them in freezer and treat your dog to 1 or 2 at a time.

See page 27 - you can also make the meat balls into Pup-Sicles!

Tested by Diane Betelak, owner of Heads & Tails
Professional Dog Grooming in Liverpool, NY, her daughter Jessica
and their standard poodle, Sid, who will be a great grooming contest dog when he grows up.
Diane is one of the American Groomers of the Year (A Cardinal Crystal Grooming Achievement Award).
Sid says: "woof, woof" (yum, yum!)

KID ALERT!

DOGS MUST BE PETTED A MINIMUM OF A MILLION TIMES A DAY!

CATS LIKE TO BE PETTED TOO. IT MAKES US PURR!

DOGS LOVE TO RUN!

BE CARING

Love Your Pet

✓ **PET CARE TIP**
Rinse your pet off after swimming in salt water or pool water.

Microwave Pup-Tarts

Ingredients:

2 c.	All Purpose or Wheat Flour
1	Large Egg
3 T.	Oatmeal or Quick Oats
1 t.	Minced Garlic or Garlic Powder
2/3 c.	Beef or Chicken Broth
	(add bouillon cube to water to get broth)

In a mixing bowl, beat egg and add broth. In a separate bowl, blend flour, oatmeal and garlic. Add liquids to dry mixture and mix well into a dough.

Form dough into a big ball. Press or roll out on a lightly floured surface until it's 1/2" thick. Cut in squares 2 x 2" and roll each square into a ball. Place balls into cupcake papers on a plate and put in a microwave with a carousel. Cook on HIGH 10 minutes or until firm. Cool until hard. Store in sandwich bags in the refrigerator.

Tested by professional groomer Diana Mohler, co-author of How Willy Got His Wheels, with her grandsons Spencer and Alex. Diana is a two-time winner of the Cardinal Crystal Grooming Achievement Award for Journalist of the Year. Her Yorkshire Terrier, Sarge, gave them his stamp of approval!

DOGS LOVE GARLIC!

BABY DOG, GO WITH ME TO THE STORE WHEN WE'RE DONE WITH THIS RECIPE?

OK, I'LL WAIT FOR YOU IN THE BARKING LOT.

A FUN THING YOU CAN DO WITH YOUR DOG:

Have a neighborhood dog show. Invite your friends and their dogs. Pick 2 judges. Decide what "ribbons" you'll award. Make sure that every dog gets some kind of award. You can have the best behaved dog, the biggest dog, the smallest dog, the best dog trick etc. Build a show ring in your backyard.

See the Crazy Dog website www.crazydog.com for instructions and patterns.

Pup-sicles

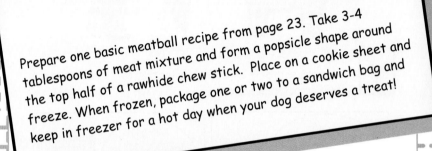

Ingredients:

Meat-O Eat-O Recipe
Rawhide Chew Sticks

Prepare one basic meatball recipe from page 23. Take 3-4 tablespoons of meat mixture and form a popsicle shape around the top half of a rawhide chew stick. Place on a cookie sheet and freeze. When frozen, package one or two to a sandwich bag and keep in freezer for a hot day when your dog deserves a treat!

✓ PET CARE TIP

Do not play with pets immediately after they eat. It's best to play with them before mealtime.

Crazy Dog's
Summer Sausage Sandwiches

Makes 2 sandwiches

Ingredients:

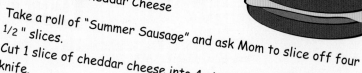

1   Pet Botanics® Dog Food Roll
1   Slice Cheddar Cheese

Take a roll of "Summer Sausage" and ask Mom to slice off four 1/2 " slices.

Cut 1 slice of cheddar cheese into 4 pieces with your spreading knife.

Take two slices of Summer Sausage and put 2 pieces of cheese in between. Repeat. You now have 2 sandwiches and you need to take your dog on a picnic!

Tested by Charlie Nanfria, 11,
Charlie's Pet Sitting and Dog Walking, Danville, CA.
"My clients love it when I bring them homemade "Crazy" treats.
Summer Sausage Sandwiches are their favorite - and they're so easy to make!"

DOGS LOVE

PICNICS

KID ALERT!

Only 2 sandwiches per day or your dog will get a tummy ache and you'll have to call the dogter.

Cat Recipes

 ## CAT CARE TIP
Cats like to do the same thing every day. They like a schedule.
They eat, they bathe, they nap, they eat, they bathe, they nap...

A FUN THING YOU CAN
DO WITH YOUR CAT:
Bird watching

Cat Nip Cocktail

Ingredients:

1 T. dried catnip (get at the pet store)
1/2 c. boiling water (microwave 1 minute on high)
1/2 c. cold water
2 ice cubes

Heat 1/2 c. of water in the microwave. Put the catnip in a tea ball and soak it in the hot water for 3 minutes. Remove tea ball. Add 1/2 c. cold water and 2 ice cubes.

Serve to your cat in a plastic martini glass at 5:00.

HOW CAN YOU CONTRIBUTE WHILE CARING FOR YOUR PET? COLLECT PET FOOD FOR YOUR LOCAL PET SHELTER -- OR VOLUNTEER AT THE SHELTER.

CATS LOVE TO SCRATCH!

CONTRIBUTE

✓ CAT CARE TIP

Catnip is adored by only about 1/2 of all cats. If your cat doesn't go "Crazy" over catnip, don't worry. For cats that do love catnip, don't give them too much. Let them play awhile, then put it away.

A FUN THING YOU CAN DO WITH YOUR CAT:
PLAY HIDE N' SEEK

You'll need to leave your kitty a little trail of snacks so she can find you. Some day when she's sleeping, spread a little trail of tiny morsels of cat treat about 1 foot apart on the floor. Make them lead to you hiding behind the chair. Then call her: "Kitty, Kitty, Kitty!" See if she can follow the trail to you!

Cheese Nips

For the laziest of cooks
Cats Love Cheese ♥

Ingredients:

6   Kitty Bite-Sized chunks of Cheddar, American or Mozzarella cheese

☑ CAT CARE TIP

Cats never drink enough water. They don't like to lap out of a bowl like dogs, so place drinking glasses of fresh water in the kitchen and the bathroom. Cats love fancy drinking glasses.

A FUN THING YOU CAN DO WITH YOUR CAT:

Hide the Catnip in the Shoe

DECORATE A
SMALL, STURDY PAPER PLATE
IN HONOR OF YOUR CAT'S BIRTHDAY.
USE MARKERS OR CRAYONS -
AND MAKE IT PRETTY!

The Quick & Easy CAT & KITTY Birthday Cake Recipe
(for even the fussiest of cats)

Take 1 small can of your cat's favorite cat food. Put it in the fridge for a couple hours. Remove the lid. Take a spreading knife and gently run the knife around the inside edge of the can, loosening the food from the can.

Put your decorated plate on top of of the cat food can. Holding the can down on the plate, quickly turn the plate over. Tap the top of the can gently with a spoon. Now carefully remove the can. Usually the food will come out in one whole piece in the shape of a can - which is like a small birthday cake.

Decorate the top with small kitty treats. Trim the outside edge with cheese in the aerosol can. (Yes, shaving cream looks better, but no you can't feed your pets shaving cream.) Serve while singing Happy Birthday!

Please note: Cats do not necessarily like parties or birthdays and are not generally known to get into the spirit of celebrations. But they do appreciate all your hard work. (It's the thought that counts.) They will love their birthday cake.

☑ PET CARE TIP

DO NOT TRIM OR CUT YOUR PET'S WHISKERS

Whiskers are one of the great "sensors" that cats and dogs have. They use their whiskers to check the air movement and air pressure. They use them to measure spaces, like to make sure they can get through the pet door. The whiskers are so sensitive that if a mouse moves through the house, the slightest movement of the air will alert a cat through its whiskers. This is especially helpful in the dark. (They're high tech!) Of course that means they know if you are out of bed when you shouldn't be.

So, if you're sneaking around in the middle of the night - you better be telling your pet and giving them a treat - or they'll tattle on you! (Especially dogs, they're the worst.)

I can't speak for dogs but cats have 4 rows of 6 whiskers (24) on each side of their face. Some ultra sensitive cats have an extra whisker. Can you count your cat's whiskers?

CATS LOVE TO SNOOP!

Tuna Quackers

Ingredients:

1/2 c.	flour
1/2 c.	powdered milk (non-fat)
1	can flaked tuna in oil
1/4 c.	water
1T.	canola oil
1	egg

Put flour and powdered milk in a medium size mixing bowl and stir. In a separate bowl put water, oil and egg. Using your cat's whisker (just kidding, use a fork) mix very well. Pour liquid into dry mix and stir! Keep stirring until you get a soft dough. Add tuna and stir well. Take a spoonful and roll into a ball. Place on a cookie sheet and flatten with your fork. Repeat until all dough is used. Bake for 10-12 minutes at 350. Remove from oven and let cool for 3-4 minutes. Take a spatula and flip the "quackers" over. Return to oven and bake another 8-10 minutes until golden brown. Cool completely. Store in sandwich bags. Serve 2 Quackers per day per cat.

CATS LOVE THEIR FAMILY

You're All Mine!
You Belong To Me...

☑ CAT CARE TIP

Cats are possessive. Cats are territorial. That means they "stake out" their own space. They "mark" their space so other cats know it's theirs. There are several ways cats "mark." They have special pheromones (scents) in their face, their footpads and their urine. When they rub up against you, they "mark" you with their own personal scent. Then other cats know you belong to them.

A FUN THING YOU CAN DO WITH YOUR CAT:

Laser Tag. Cats love chasing the small red dot from a laser light!

Mice-A-Roni Dinner

Ingredients:

2 cans	Mice (sardines or tuna if you can't find canned mice)
2/3 c.	Cooked rice
1 can	Liver Cat Food
1/4 c.	Parsley, chopped
1/2 c.	Canned Peas

Combine all ingredients and mix well. Serve half cup portions on fancy dishes. Seal and store remaining mixture in refrigerator.

Tested and approved by Muffin and Picasso, clients of Taylor's (10) Pawsitively Purrfect Petsitting, Danville, CA. Score: **"purr-fect"**

CATS LOVE A NAP

I THINK I'D LIKE SOME MICE TEA TO GO WITH MY MICE-A-RONI!

✓ CAT CARE TIP

Cats sometimes play so hard (like chasing laser lights) that they exhaust themselves. When you see they are getting tired put the toy away.

A FUN THING YOU CAN DO WITH YOUR CAT:

Play Pigs Under a Blanket: Get a little blanket or towel. Slide your hand under it and move your fingers up and down and around. Your cat will pounce and try to catch your little "piggies."

Kitty Cheese Crunchies

Ingredients:

1 1/2 c.	Wheat Flour or All Purpose Flour or mixture
1/4 c.	Nonfat Dry Milk Powder
1/2 c.	Cheddar Cheese, grated
1/2 c.	Parmesan cheese, grated
3 T.	Canola Oil
2 t.	Garlic Salt
1/2 c.	Water

Mix cheeses and oil in a large bowl. Add flour, milk powder and garlic salt and water, blend until dough forms and is slightly stiff. Flour surface and roll out dough to 1/2" thickness. Cut in small squares about the size of a Chex cereal. Lightly grease a cookie sheet and spread squares on sheet. Bake 7-9 minutes at 350 degrees. Removed from oven and turn over with a spatula. Return to oven and bake another 7-9 minutes.

Tested by Deborah Rowe,
professional groomer, trainer and customer
service representative for Cardinal Laboratories Inc.
Her Siamese cat Bailey said they are "meow-valous"!

CAT CARE TIP
Cats bathe and groom themselves many times a day. Don't put anything on their fur that might make them sick when they lick it.

A FUN THING YOU CAN DO WITH YOUR CAT:

Plant catnip in the garden or in an outside flowerpot. It grows quickly. Then your cat can help you pick the leaves! You can put the leaves in a sandwich bag and store them in the freezer for year 'round treats.

Cat Fish Cakes:
Tuna Treats
Makes about 240 pieces
Preparation time: 20 minutes Cooking time: 15 minutes

Ingredients:

1/2 c. wheat flour
1/4 c. corn meal
1/4 c. cottage cheese
1 can tuna

Put tuna and cottage cheese in a mixing bowl. Stir in cornmeal and wheat flour mix until a soft dough forms. Roll into a ball then roll out to 1/4-inch thickness on a floured surface. Cut dough into 3/4-inch squares and place on greased cookie sheet. Bake at 350 degrees for 12-15 minutes. Cool before giving to pet. Store in sandwich bags in refrigerator.

✓ CAT CARE TIP

Cats sleep a lot, especially after they eat. Older cats sleep more than younger ones. House cats sleep more than outdoor cats. Do not bother them when they're "cat napping."

HAVE RESPECT

A FUN THING YOU CAN DO WITH YOUR CAT:

Hang a bird feeder outside a window where you and your cat can sit and watch the birds. While your cat is busy "stalking" the birds, you can learn to recognize different kinds of birds.

Canary Feathers

Ingredients:

1 1/2 c.	Wheat Flour	3 T.	Vegetable Oil
2 T.	Wheat Germ	1/3 c.	Milk
1/3 c.	Powdered Milk	1/4 t.	Yellow food coloring
1 T.	Molasses	1 t.	Catnip
1	Egg		(buy at the pet shop)

Put flour, wheat germ and powdered milk in a large bowl. Add molasses, egg, oil, milk and food color. Mix well to form a dough. Roll out flat on floured surface. Cut into small pieces (the size of canary feathers) and bake on a greased cookie sheet at 350 degrees for 20 minutes.

Prepared by Vyra Pacheco,
CPA, and approved by Diesel, her registered
Bengal cat. "Diesel and I are very "purr-snickety" about what
he eats. He loves the Canary Feathers taste and I like the nutrition."

MY COUSIN SOCKS WAS SUPPOSED TO COME VISIT BUT SHE NEVER SHOWED UP.

SOCKS? WHY'D THEY NAME HER SOCKS?

SHE ACCIDENTALLY GOT SHUT IN THE DRYER AND WE NEVER SAW HER AGAIN.

I'D HAVE CALLED HER FLUFFY!

✓ CAT CARE TIP

Cats like to be talked to. They like to know what you did today, where you've been and who you saw. They're very curious. They will sniff you to see if they can smell where you've been and if another pet came near you! You might as well tell. (They're good at keeping secrets!)

A FUN THING YOU CAN DO WITH YOUR CAT:

The Ol' Paper Bag Game

Take a paper grocery or shopping bag and put it on the floor for your cat to play in - they love paper bags. For extra fun, tie a string to the back of the bag and every time your cat starts to crawl in, pull it!

Bird Nests

Ingredients:

1 c   Cooked Chicken, chopped in small bits
1/4 c   Fresh cooked broccoli, chopped
1/4 c   Shredded cooked carrots
1/4 c.   Canned peas
2T.   Chicken broth

Mix all ingredients together,
serve in cup cake papers.

CATS LOVE PAPER BAGS

WHAT DID THE 500 POUND CANARY SAY?

"HERE, KITTY, KITTY..."

?

500 lbs. SCARY!

Important Pet Food Tips You Should Know

 Dogs and Cats **CANNOT** eat Chocolate!

 Dogs and Cats **CANNOT** eat Onions!

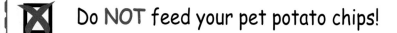 Do **NOT** feed your pet potato chips!

Do **NOT** feed your pet chicken or turkey bones!

Measurements & Tools We Use

Cooking Measurements we use in the book:

t. = teaspoon
T. = tablespoon
c. = cup

Tools We Use in this book:

 Hot Pads or Oven Mitts

 Mixing bowls

 Measuring spoons

 Measuring cup

 Spreading knife - not sharp

 Cookie Sheet

 Cupcake Tin

 Sandwich Bags

 Whiskers (Mixing Spoons)

Crazy Cat's Rules For Cooking

- ## Wash Your Hands
  - ► Before You Start
  - ► Every time you lick your fingers
  - ► After You're Finished

Crazy Cat's Rules For Cooking

DAHLINGS, YOU MUST FOLLOW THE RULES, IT IS ESSENTIAL TO BEING A GOOD CHEF!

BE FAIR

FOLLOWING THE RULES IS PART OF BEING FAIR

#1 Ask Your Mom if you can cook

- ► Put on an apron or a big T-shirt to protect your clothes

- ► Wash Your Hands

- ► Don't Lick Your Fingers and Put them Back in the Bowl

- ► Do Not Throw Food

- ► Clean Up When You're Done - Yep, Wash Those Dishes

- ► Don't Use Knives Without Supervision

A DAY AT THE CAT SPA:

Giving Your Kitty A Total Beauty Treatment

Dahlings, there's nothing a cat likes better than a day at the spa. If you want to properly care for your cat, a weekly appointment at the salon is imperative. It's very easy to set up your own home salon if you aren't near my Crazy Cat Spa & Grooming Parlor. (Besides, we're completely booked. No one ever misses an appointment at my shop.) A full day of beauty for your cat should include the following treatments:

PET-I-CURES

You can lightly file the nails with a light emery board. If your kitty likes polish and your Mom approves you can carefully paint the toes.

Nail clipping is the one thing that should be done by an adult. It needs to be done at least monthly. Ask your groomer to teach your Mom or Dad how to clip nails.

If your kitty doesn't like to have it's nails done, you can line the bottom of a scratching box with light sand paper and kitty can give herself her own Pet-I-Cure every time she scratches.

EYE CLEANING

Soak a cotton ball with lukewarm water and gently wipe the eye area

EAR EXAM

Wash the ears with a damp cloth. Very gently clean out wax with a swab. Look for ear mites or ticks in the ear. They look like little black spots. If you find them, you need a product called Ear Mite and Tick Control®.

FULL BODY BRUSH

Brush your kitty thoroughly from head to tail – at least 10 times. Now brush under the chin. Redo the top of her head. Now turn her over and gently brush her tummy.

MASSAGE

Using your hands as a brush, start at the head and massage to the tip of the tail. Reverse and go from the tip of the tail to the head. Then go from the head to the tail again. Using your fingers, massage the head and make strokes down the legs. Rub the pads of her feet making a circular motion. Be gentle!

THE FINISHING TOUCHES

Using a fine-toothed comb, carefully comb your kitty's fur back into place. If it's time for her monthly flea drop, ask Mom to do it now. Add a touch of your favorite fragrance behind the ears and on the tip of the tail.

Don't forget to make her next appointment before she leaves your shop!

The Purr-fessional Pet Owners Purr-fect Pet Care Chart for Purr-snickity Cats

Do these things with your pet every day for 21 days and you will become the Purr-fect Pet Owner.

 Morning:
- Feed Your Cat When You Have Breakfast
- Put Fresh Water In the Water Dish or Glass
- Kiss Your Kitty Good-by When You Go to School

 Afternoon:
- Give Your Kitty a Treat When You Have Your Afternoon Snack (Make it a Crazy Cat snack!)
- Clean the Litter Box
- Play A Game With Kitty

 Evening:
- Feed Your Cat When You Have Dinner
- Brush your cat while you tell it everything you've done today.

BE DEPENDABLE

The Divine Dog Owners
"Do This" Dog Care Diagram

Do these things with your dog every day for 21 days and you will become a Divine Dog Owner - and best friend of your dog!

Morning:
- Let Your Dog Outside to go potty as soon as you get up (Guess who gets to pick up after him – you!)
- Feed your dog at the same time every morning, then let him outside again to do his duty.
- Put Fresh Water in the Dog Bowl before you go to school.
- Say Good-bye before you leave for school

Afternoon:
- Greet your dog with whistles, "hey-boys," hugs and kisses when you come home from school.
- Take your dog outside as soon as you get home from school.
- Give your dog a treat when you have your afternoon snack.
- Make sure it's a Crazy Dog snack - I didn't write this cookbook for nothing!
- Take your dog for a walk and play with him.

Evening:
- Feed your dog when you have dinner.
- Let the dog out after he eats.
- Brush him before you go to bed.

Sometimes it takes courage to go home and feed and walk your dog when you'd rather go play.

HAVE COURAGE

If you don't have time to cook you can buy these treats at your favorite pet store!

Crazy Bitz Peanut Butter Nuggets: Pretzel with Peanut Butter Inside But No Salt on the Outside

Crazy Dog Train Me! Training Reward Bacon Flavored

DOGS LOVE

All of these

Crazy Dog Train Me! Training Reward Chicken Flavored

Crazy Dog Train Me! Training Reward Liver Flavored

CATS

Coming Soon! Crazy Cat Treats!

www.crazypetpress.com

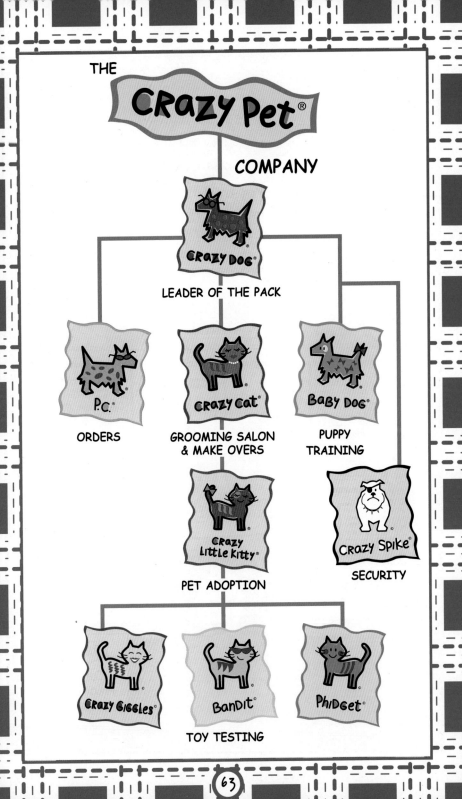

THE

CRaZy Pet®

COMPANY

CRaZy DOG®

LEADER OF THE PACK

P.C.®

ORDERS

CRaZy Cat®

GROOMING SALON
& MAKE OVERS

BaBy DOG®

PUPPY
TRAINING

CRaZy Little kitty®

PET ADOPTION

CRaZy Spike®

SECURITY

CRaZy Giggles®

BanDit®

PhiDget®

TOY TESTING